Introduction

by Tim Allen

Abingdon Abbey was one of the largest and wealthiest in England, and dominated the life (and skyline) of the town for over 800 years. The monastery's building programme for the church rarely stopped throughout all that time! Due to the very thorough demolition after the dissolution of the abbey by Henry VIII, however, few abbey buildings remain, and the physical, as well as the spiritual and economic, domination of the abbey is now difficult to imagine.

The surviving buildings are already described in the guidebook by the Friends of Abingdon. The history of Abingdon Abbey has also been dealt with in the studies of the ancient charters and the Cartuleries, and in Mieneke Cox's more anecdotal, but exceedingly informative, histories. We do not intend to go over the same ground.

The influence of Abingdon Abbey upon the town, and vice versa, has however become clearer through archaeological investigations in the last 30 years. Abingdon Abbey was also the greatest medieval landowner in Berkshire, and traces of this are still present around the town and in the wider landscape.

This booklet presents discoveries from excavations in the abbey precinct, and the plans from successive geophysical surveys since 1998, which have provided a much more detailed plan of the church, and enabled the first well-founded reconstructions of its development. It also aims to give a taste of the very wide-ranging activities of the abbey as landowner, employer and power in the town.

1989 excavations of belltower and lay cemetery

Before the Abbey

Iron Age decorated bowl

Abingdon may be the earliest continuously occupied town in England. There was an extensive settlement here at the start of the Iron Age (around 700 BC), which continued up to and beyond the Roman conquest in AD 43

In the last years BC the settlement was defended by multiple ditches up to 12 m wide and nearly 3 m deep, first identified under the present Waitrose site in Station Yard, and later found south of the Square and in West St Helen Street car park. The defensive line curved from the river Ock up to the river Stert on the north, and then south-east back towards the Thames. The spoil was used to create a large rampart behind the innermost ditch. Peat in the ditch bottoms shows that they were permanently waterlogged, in effect moats.

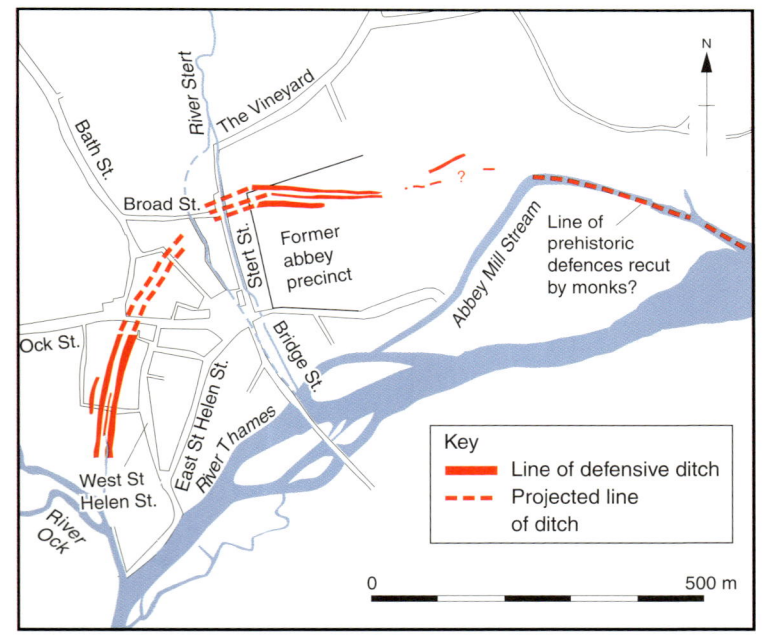

East of Waitrose car park the ditches have not been traced, but the abbey mill stream (dug by abbot Aethelwold and his monks) may well have followed the ancient defences at the east end, as the line of the mill stream kinks suddenly.

The defences enclosed an area of around 20 hectares. Excavations stretching from West St Helen Street to Abbey House and Waitrose have shown that everywhere inside there was dense settlement and crafts including metalworking. Hints of a regular layout suggest central authority, in other words a riverside proto-town.

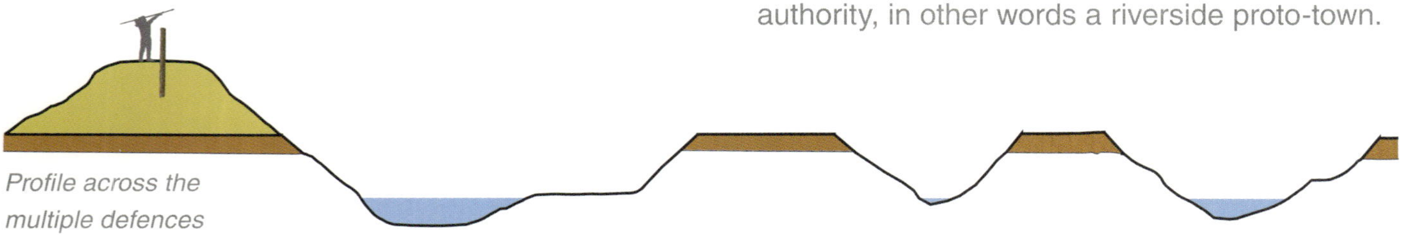

Profile across the multiple defences

Survival of the defences

Dense occupation continued through the Roman period and into Saxon times. Roman stone buildings have been found under Abbey House, in the Old Gaol and East St Helen Street, and pagan Saxon houses and finds under Abbey House car park and the High Street

Part of the rampart and inner ditch on the north was levelled in Roman times (see bank levelling in photo of ditch section below), but most of the defences silted up over many centuries.

South of Ock Street the inner ditch was recut in the medieval period. It ran down the back of the properties west of West St Helen Street, and explains the curve of West St Helen Street today, though the rampart is long gone. The ditch survived beyond AD 1848, when it was marked on the Christ's Hospital map (the earliest detailed town map). It was called the Shitebourne, a testament to the lack of a proper sewerage system until Victorian times!

The defences have not been excavated between the Square and Stert Street, but a curving line of small plots linking the known ancient defences marks their line. 16th century references to `the cleaning of the town ditch' here show that a ditch still existed then. Bury Street was formerly Littlebridge Street, perhaps referring to a bridge over the defences at its north end.

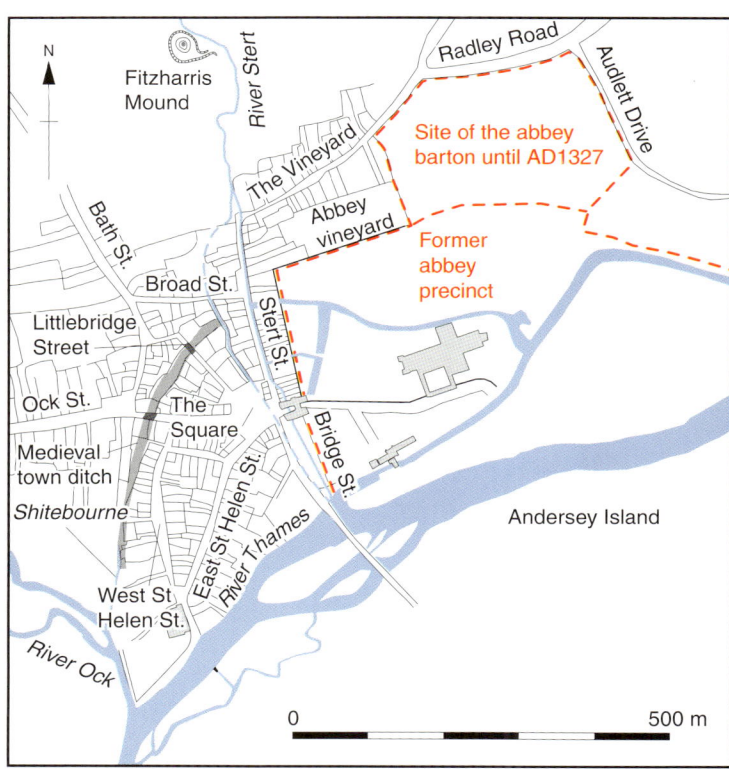

Bank levelled back into ditch

The early abbey – legend or history?

The foundation stories of Abingdon abbey suggest that a monastery dedicated to St Mary and a nunnery dedicated to St Helen were established in the 7th century by a brother and sister, Hean and Cilla. The two sit in opposite corners of the ancient defences. Double foundations (one for monks and one for nuns) did occur elsewhere, for instance at Whitby and Hartlepool, at this time. The Abingdon Chronicle says that the ancient buildings of the this first abbey were mostly in ruins when Aethelwold arrived from Glastonbury in AD 953 to refound it.

Unfortunately, the charters used by the medieval abbey to back up its ancient pedigree mostly belonged to a church at Bradfield near Reading, and may have been brought to Abingdon abbey by Aethelwold to bolster its reputation. The only archaeological evidence of 7th-9th century activity at Abingdon, at the abbey or in the town, consists of a handful of metal objects, including the Black Cross found by Aethelwold's monks and drawn in the 13th century. St Helens and much of the abbey site however remain unexcavated, and it is likely that a religious house of some sort remains to be discovered.

From Aethelwold onwards, the history of the abbey is well-documented. The Witan (the king's council) met on Andersey Island twice in the 10th century, and there was possibly a royal hunting lodge there. The decision to establish the church of St Helen, and the monastery of St Mary, was probably influenced by the defensive position provided by the ancient defences, by the stonework available in the Roman buildings, and by the royal residence on Andersey Island.

Drawing of the Black cross, a ring-headed decorative 8th century pin

Strap end with animal head and interlacing ornament

Benedictine Monasticism and Abingdon Abbey

Monastic Christian communities were founded to enable men and women to seek God through a life of self-discipline and prayer. Many early monks, including St Benedict (AD 480-c. 550) were solitary hermits dwelling in remote places, but they attracted many followers, creating communities of worship, protection, and mutual support. His Rule for the conduct of monastic life was adopted in AD 816 for all of the Catholic world, and is still the most influential in Western Christianity.

Benedict understood the monastery to be 'a school of the Lord's service', and he wrote his Rule for ordinary people of varied abilities. His counsels were `to build up the weak but also to spur on the strong, so that all might climb the ladder of perfection according to their abilities'. This required stability (commitment to the community), conversion of manners (spiritual transformation according to the pattern of Jesus Christ), and obedience (freedom from self-will being a pathway to God). Monks were to retain no personal possessions.

The Rule also provides for the election of the abbot, the appointment of officials, the round of daily living, the provision of hospitality (guests should 'be welcomed as Christ himself'), and advice for reconciling conflict. The purpose of the community is the opus Dei, the hours spent in prayer day and night. Benedict envisaged about four hours of communal prayer, the same of private prayer and spiritual reading, and six hours of manual labour every day.

The Abingdon Missal or Mass Book, AD 1416 (MS Digby 227, fol. 113v courtesy of the Bodleian Library)

In the early middle ages monks were spiritual soldiers, who fought against supernatural enemies. The monastery was a spiritual `castle', and benefactors conferred gifts of land and money so that monks might pray for their eternal welfare. For the nobility, to be a monk was a respected calling, and monks often held the highest positions in church and state.

Monasteries were focuses for employment, craftsmanship, and artistic, musical and technical innovation and excellence. Abbot (later St) Aethelwold (AD 953-963) was himself a leading statesman, scholar and teacher. With St Dunstan of Canterbury and St Oswald of Worcester, he led the revival and reform of Benedictine monasticism in England. He wrote the Regularis Concordia setting out the timetable of daily prayer, introduced the Abbey of Fleury's chant technique to Britain, installed an organ and supervised the founding of bells. His church at Abingdon was furnished with stone sculpture and gold and silver metalwork, and he was also responsible for works of civil engineering like the digging of the millstream.

Pilgrims sought out the miracle-working relics kept at monasteries. Abingdon's best-known were those of St Vincent of Saragossa (the first Spanish martyr) and the 'Black Cross' of Abingdon, reportedly fashioned from a nail of the True Cross.

For much of the medieval period, Abingdon Abbey was the only provider of alms (charity) to the poor, of medical care to the sick (through St John's Hospital), and of education (the abbey's school later became Abingdon School). Through monastic schools poor boys of ability could sometimes rise to high office. In a largely illiterate society, monastic libraries preserved the knowledge of classical antiquity and even of the Islamic world for succeeding generations.

The Monastic Horarium for summer according to Aethelwold's Regularis Concordia

1.30 am	Rise
	Trina oratio – gradual psalms
2 am	NOCTURNS – psalms
3.30-4 am	MATINS
	Miserere, Psalms for Royal House,
	Anthems, Matins of All Saints in porticu
	Change and wash
5 am	Reading
6 am	PRIME
	Psalms and prayers, etc.
	MORROW MASS
	Chapter meeting
7.30 am	Work
8 am	TERCE – sung mass
	Five psalms for the dead, etc
9.30 am	Reading
c. 9.45 am	Work
11.30 am	SEXT – sung mass
	Psalms, etc., for Royal House
12 noon	Dinner
1 pm	Siesta
2.30 pm	NONE
	Psalms, etc., for Royal House
	Drink
3 pm	Work
5.30 pm	Supper
6 pm	VESPERS
	Psalms and Anthems,
	Vespers of All Saints and the Dead
7.30 pm	Change into night shoes, Collatio
8 pm	COMPLINE – Trina oratio
8.15 pm	Bed

The Great Work

Monastic churches were built `for the glory of God', so their size and magnificence reflected not only the numbers of recruits joining monasteries, but also the devotion of those who built them. Successive abbots each wanted to add something of their own. There was also competition among abbeys to be chosen as the resting place of the rich and powerful, and thus to obtain grants of land and other marks of patronage for masses to be said for the dead in perpetuity.

The abbey documents surviving from medieval times, which include chronicles of the lives of the abbots, make occasional reference to their building campaigns. There is also a selection of the yearly accounts of the senior monks (called Obedientiaries) running different parts of the abbey's administration (see also page 18). These show that the enlargement or rebuilding of the abbey church was virtually continuous throughout the medieval period.

This means that the abbey church contained numerous additions, each in the architectural style of the time. Despite an extensive facelift in the 15th century in the nave and at the west end, it is likely that the church displayed a variety of architectural styles further east, like the surviving cathedrals at Canterbury, Gloucester and Lincoln.

Secondly, it means that teams of stonemasons, carpenters, smiths, carters, ropemakers, and glaziers, would have had constant employment over hundreds of years. Many of these would have settled in the town, bringing their craft skills to the town as well, and creating employment for others who serviced their needs.

View of what the 16th century west front may have been like (Wells Cathedral projected onto the Abbey Gardens)

Previous evidence of the abbey church

Abingdon Abbey was dissolved by King Henry VIII in AD 1538, and all but one church tower had been demolished by AD 1580. The two 16th century `maps' of Abingdon are later than the Dissolution, and both concentrate on the river Thames, as they concerned fishing disputes. The Monks' Map (on the right) appeared to show the church overpainted, but infra red reflectology (by Tager Stonor Richardson) has not revealed anything more.

Our best eyewitness is William of Worcester, who visited Abingdon in the late 15th century, wrote a description and measured the church. He gave the length of the. He said that nave as 60 yards, the choir and St Mary's Chapel 66 yards. The historian Leland, who saw the church before its' demolition, stated that the central tower, the nave and the two west towers had all been built under four 15th century abbots. The west end of Abingdon Abbey church therefore probably looked like Wells Cathedral.

Monks' Map (Copyright Abingdon Town Council)

In 1922 over 30 trenches were excavated across the church and cloister. The excavation was funded and directed by A E Preston, with advice from Sir Alfred Peers and Sir Arthur Clapham. Most of the recording fell to Preston's secretary, Miss Agnes Baker, and to the surveyor, Charles Overy. The results remained

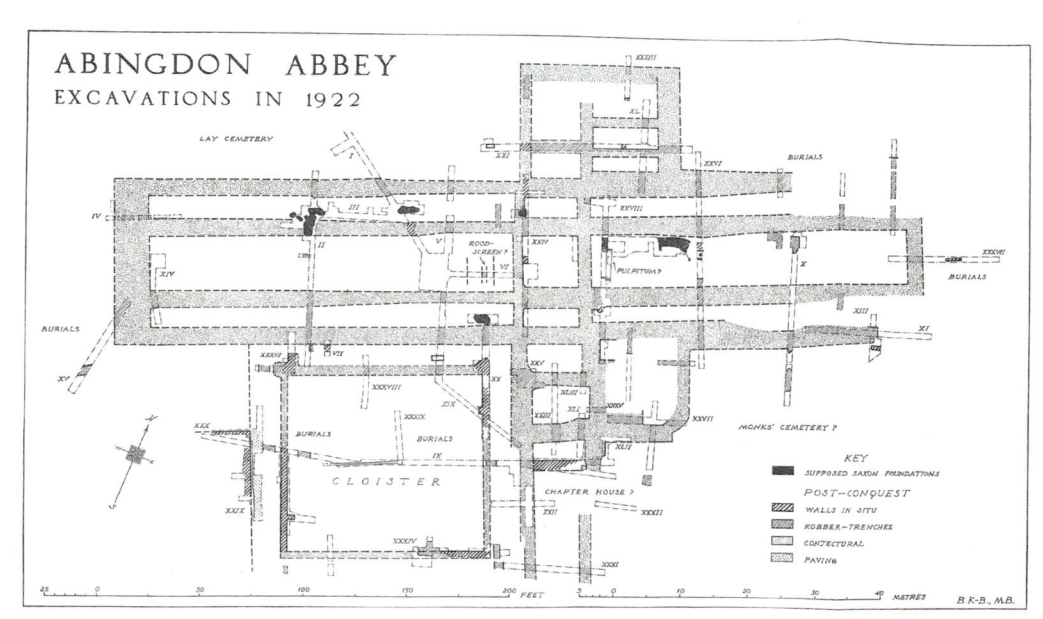

Plan of the Abbey church (Copyright Martin Biddle, published Medieval Archaeology 1968)

unpublished until 1968, when Martin Biddle reconstructed and published a plan of the church. Nevertheless, details are few, and the plan contained only the barest bones of the layout. It was believed that the abbey church had been very thoroughly demolished, so that almost nothing remained.

The 1989 excavations and the resistivity survey

In 1989 Oxford Archaeology excavated the lay cemetery and its belltower north-west of the abbey church (see page 16) in advance of the construction of new District Council Offices (Abbey House). Since then, successive geophysical surveys have been carried out to obtain a more detailed understanding of the abbey church. This work, by Bartlett-Clark Geophysics, was funded by two Heritage Lottery grants, the first for magnetometer and resistivity surveys in 1998 and 2001 as part of the restoration of the Abbey Gardens, the second ground radar and resistivity profiling surveys for this booklet.

Agnes Baker and the Saxon apse

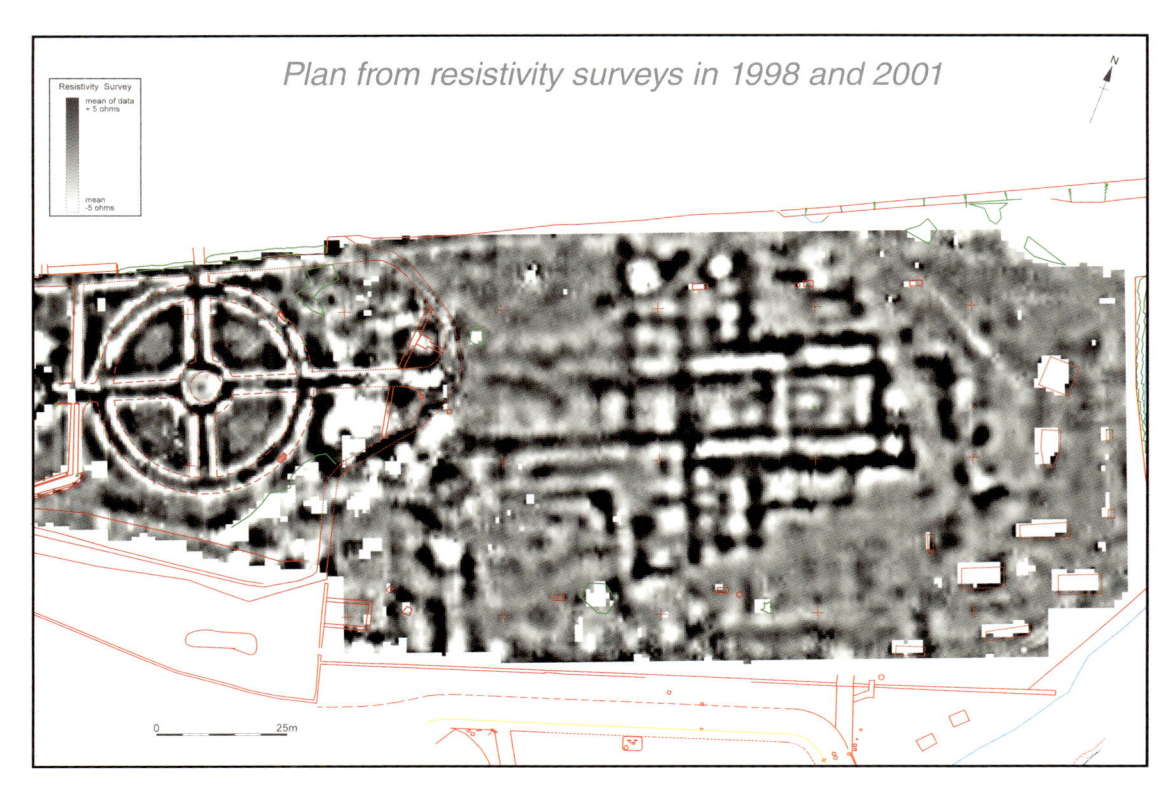

Plan from resistivity surveys in 1998 and 2001

The west end of the church is obscured

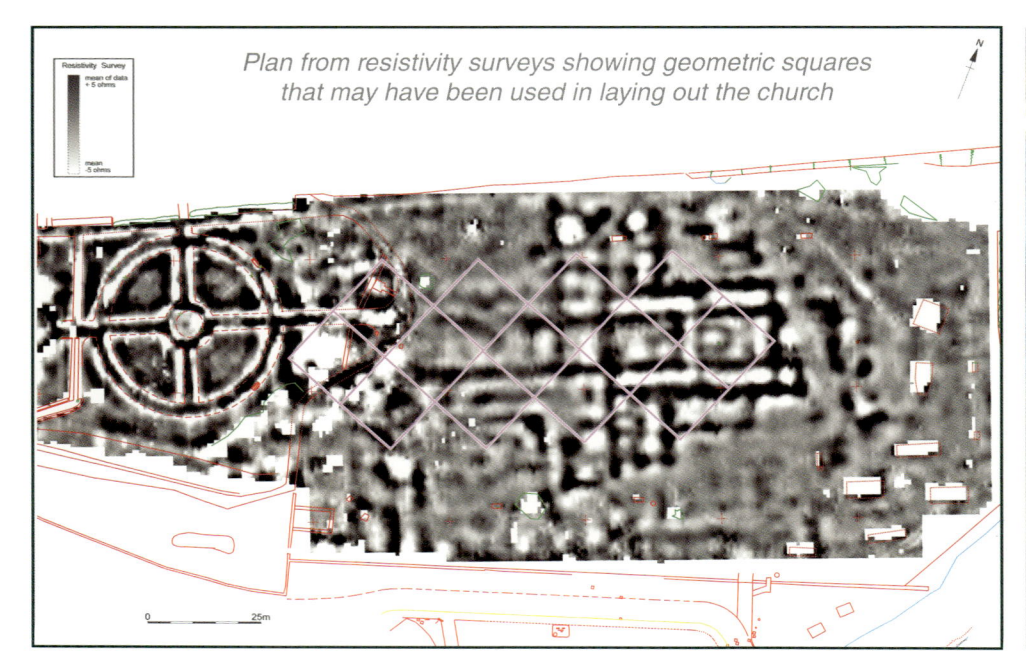

Plan from resistivity surveys showing geometric squares that may have been used in laying out the church

The lay cemetery during excavation

by the trees and bushes separating the formal garden from the grassed area, and by the metal used in the formal garden. Churches were however laid out (and extended) to precise geometric designs. Overlaying such a design on the plan places the west end of the church where the survey and the 1922 excavations tentatively suggest it should be.

The resistivity survey provided a much more detailed plan, suggesting a series of enlargements. These are however foundations rather than walls and the two did not always correspond precisely. Also as the survey shows all

Provisional interpretation of the resistivity survey

10

phases of building at once interpretation is not straightforward. Nevertheless, where walls stop against others, we can plausibly suggest that they were added later, and we have supported our conclusions with a general knowledge of the development of standing medieval churches and cathedrals.

Radar survey

The resistivity survey provided only a snapshot of the buried foundations at one depth, so we commissioned a ground radar survey to recover a series of plans at different depths. This has helped fill in some gaps in the resistivity survey, and has given a much clearer view of the deeper foundations. It has, for instance, clarified the pillar foundations in the transepts, and has also helped confirm the outline of the Saxon apse found in the 1922 excavations.

Radar 'slice' showing the buried features at a depth of c.1.8m

Any interpretation based only on survey and very old excavations can only be tentative. The new surveys have also raised new questions and suggested lines of further investigation, particularly for the Saxon period, which cannot currently be answered.

Here we have attempted to separate the plan into a series of phases, and to link these to the brief documentary references to building campaigns by various abbots, and through them, to the succession of different styles of architecture in medieval times. For each phase, a plausible interpretative plan has been superimposed on the surveys, and used as the basis for a 3-dimensional reconstruction, taking into account information from the documentary sources.

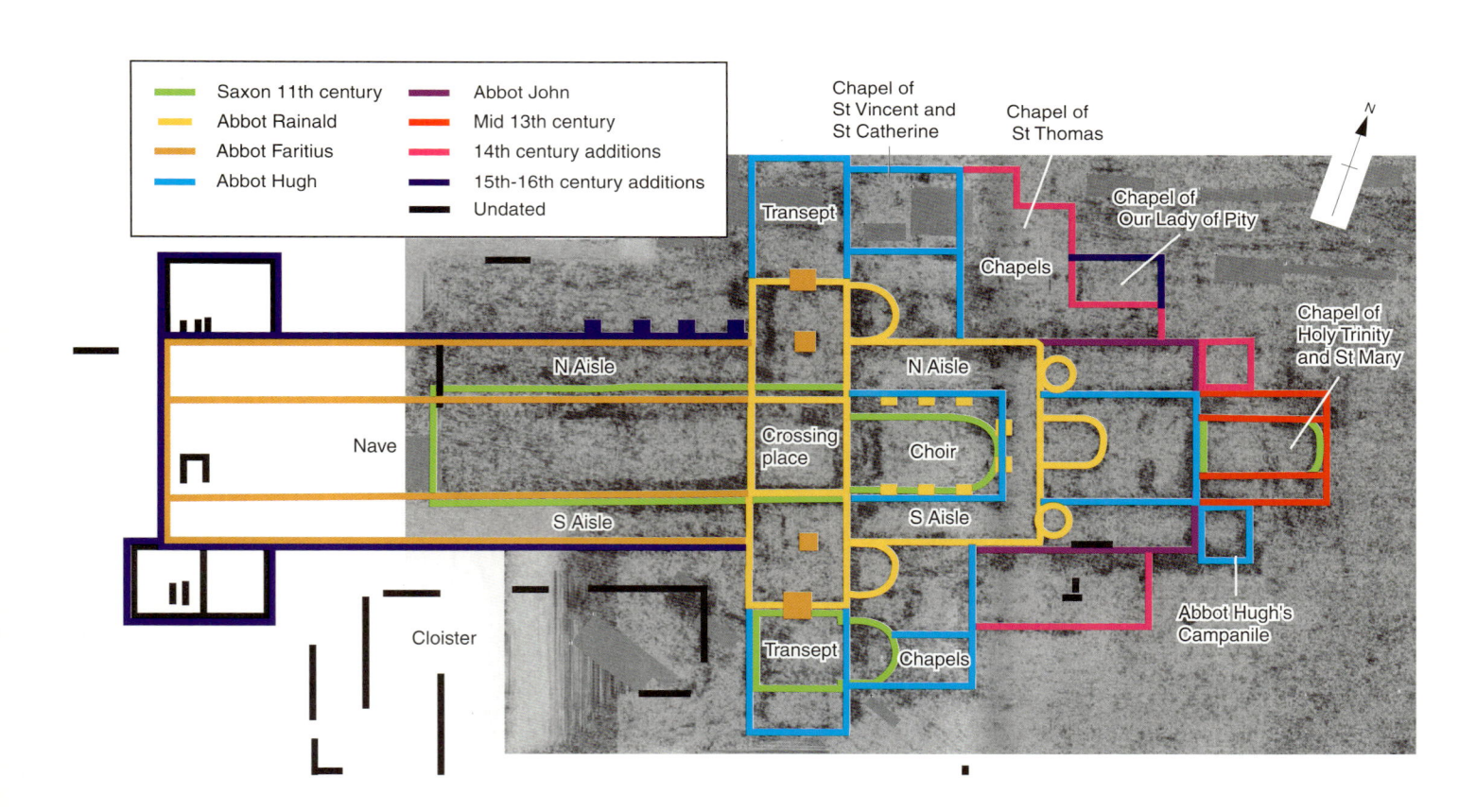

The late Saxon abbey church

Saxon churches, like that still surviving at Bradford-on-Avon, were usually long and thin, without aisles. We know from documents that a small chapel existed on the north side, but we have not been able to identify this on the surveys.

The apsidal (round-ended) chancel here is like the one that Aethelwold built at Winchester, where he became bishop after he left Abingdon. The foundations of this were found in the 1922 excavations (see plan and photo on page 9), and the outline was confirmed by the radar survey.

We know that the church had a central tower because Abbot Rainald (AD 1084-1096) began work extending the east end of the church soon after the Norman conquest. He had the east chapel next to the tower removed, but as a result the tower fell down in AD 1091 and so much of the church had to be rebuilt. The circular shape of the tower is an interpretation based upon the medieval description, and rises from a square base. This description is however very like that of the 7th century church at Abingdon, so there may have been some confusion, and the late Saxon tower may in fact have been square.

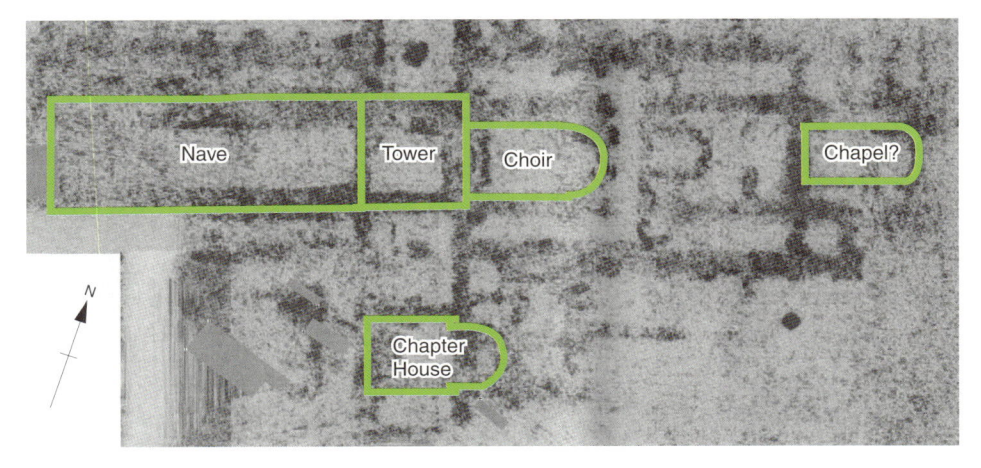

Another possible apse-ended building lies at the very east end of the church plan. If the survey is correct, this could have been a second Saxon church in line with the first, a common feature on important monastic sites. Such churches were often incorporated or swallowed by the expansion of the medieval church, as might have happened here. This is however unconfirmed, so is not shown in the reconstruction.

13

The Norman abbey church

After the tower collapsed, the church was completely rebuilt under abbots Rainald, Faritius and Vincent. Rainald built and rededicated the choir, always the first part of the church to be built or enlarged. The monks then slept in the choir while the cloister, including their dormitory, was rebuilt.

Faritius (AD 1100-1117) built the nave, two towers, most of the central tower and a chapel to Mary Magdalene. Vincent (AD 1121-1130) completed the central tower and provided new bells. All these were in the Romanesque style (round-headed doors and windows, and vertical raised strips down the outside). Faritius' two towers were probably at the E corners. Semicircular projections east of the transepts were probably chapels.

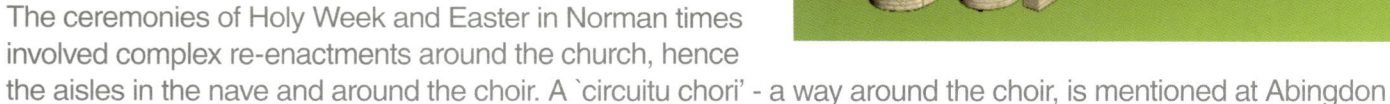

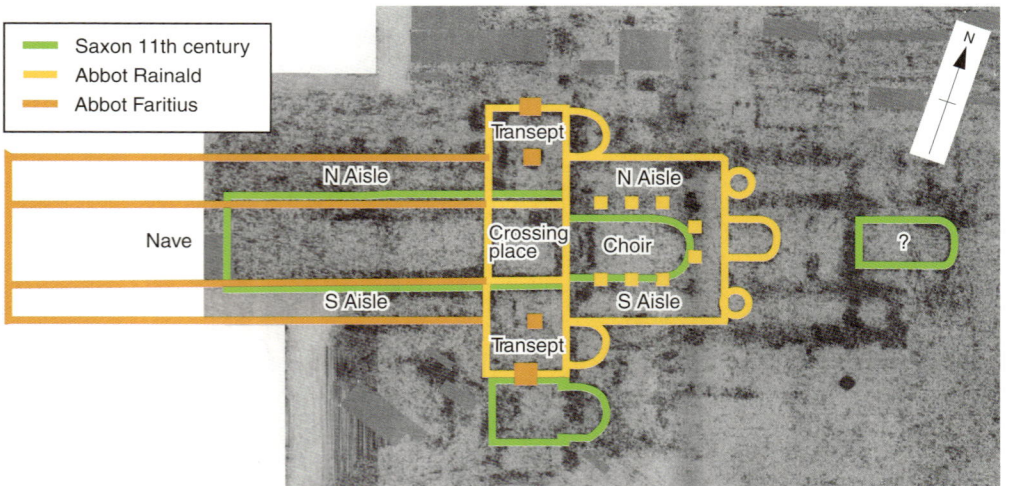

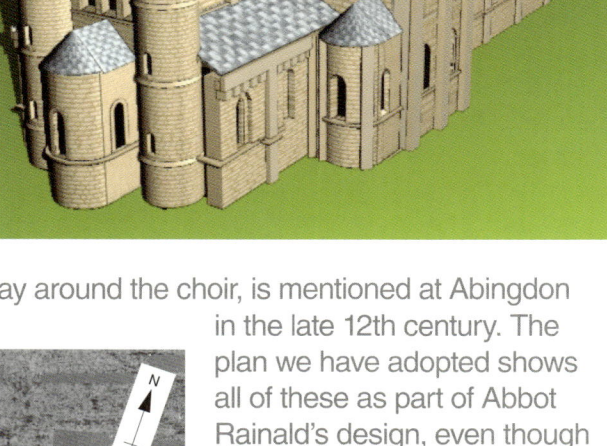

The ceremonies of Holy Week and Easter in Norman times involved complex re-enactments around the church, hence the aisles in the nave and around the choir. A `circuitu chori' - a way around the choir, is mentioned at Abingdon in the late 12th century. The plan we have adopted shows all of these as part of Abbot Rainald's design, even though it took generations to complete this work.

The radar survey has revealed massive pits along the lines of the aisles on either side of the crossing place. These were probably for pillars like those at Canterbury Cathedral built in AD1070.

Late 12th/13th century improvements

Abbot Hugh (AD 1189-1221) planned and began extensive additions to the church, including transepts, aisles, and a bell-tower to the east. The `new work' would have been in the new Gothic style, with pointed windows and doors. The work was continued by Abbot John (AD 1241-56), who completed the aisles and added the chapel of St Mary and of the Holy Trinity at the east end.

We have interpreted this as the major extension of the east end, nearly doubling the length of the choir and the aisles alongside it, extending the transepts north and south, and adding chapels on the east side. The new bell-tower was at the south-east corner of the extended church.

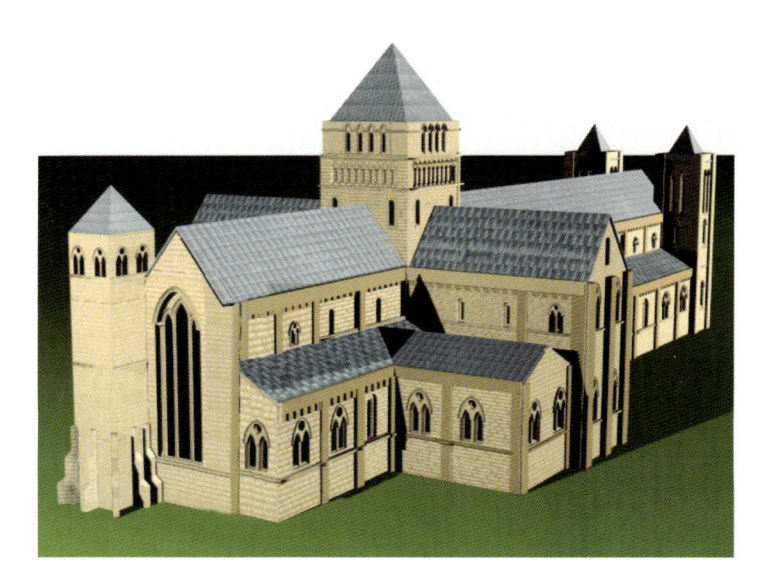

The surveys of the north transept are not very clear, perhaps due to particularly extensive robbing, but there are sufficient massive foundations to reconstruct them as symmetrical on north and south.

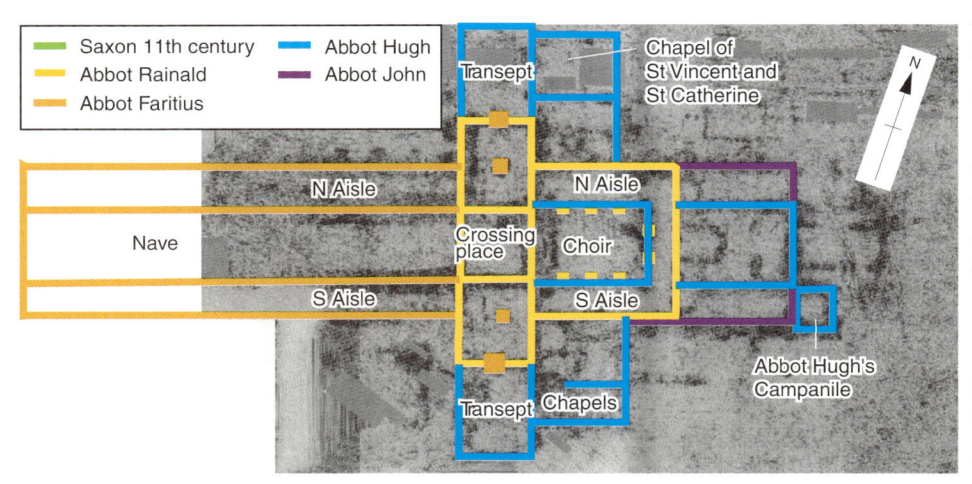

Abbot John also built the chapel of the Holy Cross, St Edmund (of Abingdon) and St Guthlac in the lay cemetery, and was perhaps also responsible for enclosing the wooden bell-frame there with an octagonal buttressing wall. The foundations of both were found in the excavations under Abbey House (see page 16). The 13th century octagonal tower must have looked like the surviving medieval bell-tower at Pembridge in Herefordshire (see page 29).

15

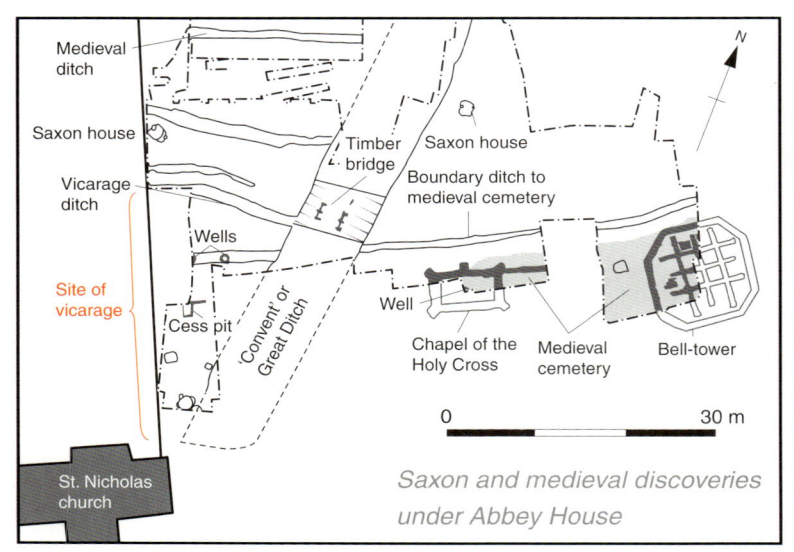

Saxon and medieval discoveries under Abbey House

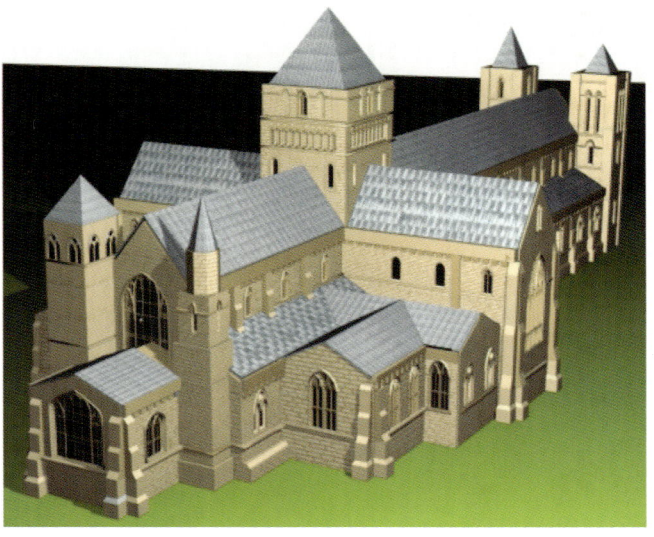

Later 13th/14th century additions

Abbot John also added the chapel of St Mary and the Trinity at the east end of the church. This came after the main extension planned by Abbot Hugh, so is shown here. Around AD 1300 a new aisle was added, probably that south of Abbot Hugh's extension to the choir. Documents also mention a chapel of St Thomas the Martyr in the N part of the church. These additions would have been in the ornate Decorated style.

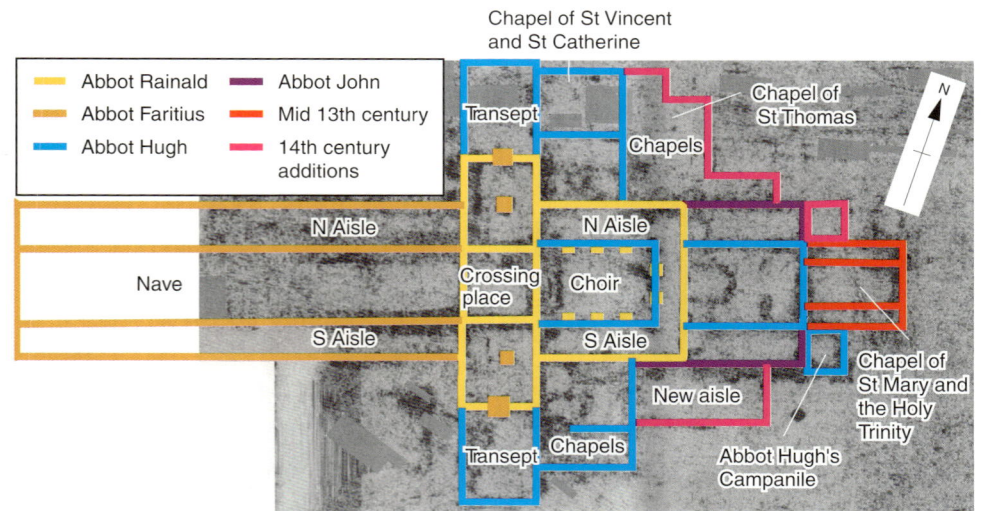

Neither of the survey techniques provided very clear results on the north; the resistivity survey suggests that there may have been a similar aisle on the north, and a shorter extension beyond that, but the radar survey suggests a separate, free-standing building.

The radar survey did not reveal significant foundations at the NE corner of the church, but the resistivity survey showed a large signal where the corner of a square tower matching the belltower on the SE would have been. We have interpreted this as another tower added opposite Abbot Hugh's belltower at this time.

15th and 16th century changes

According to Leland, the central tower, the body of the church (which we take to be the nave and its aisles) and both of the towers at the west end were built by four 15th century abbots (Salford AD 1427-8; Hamme AD 1428-35; Ashenden AD 1436-68, and Sante AD 1468-96). Rather than built, this probably meant rebuilding in the new, Perpendicular style of architecture, with its vertical ribs running the full height of the windows, and more elaborate decoration on the towers.

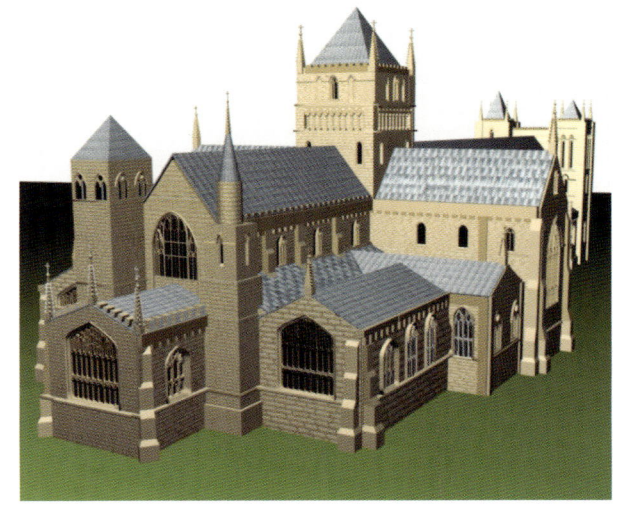

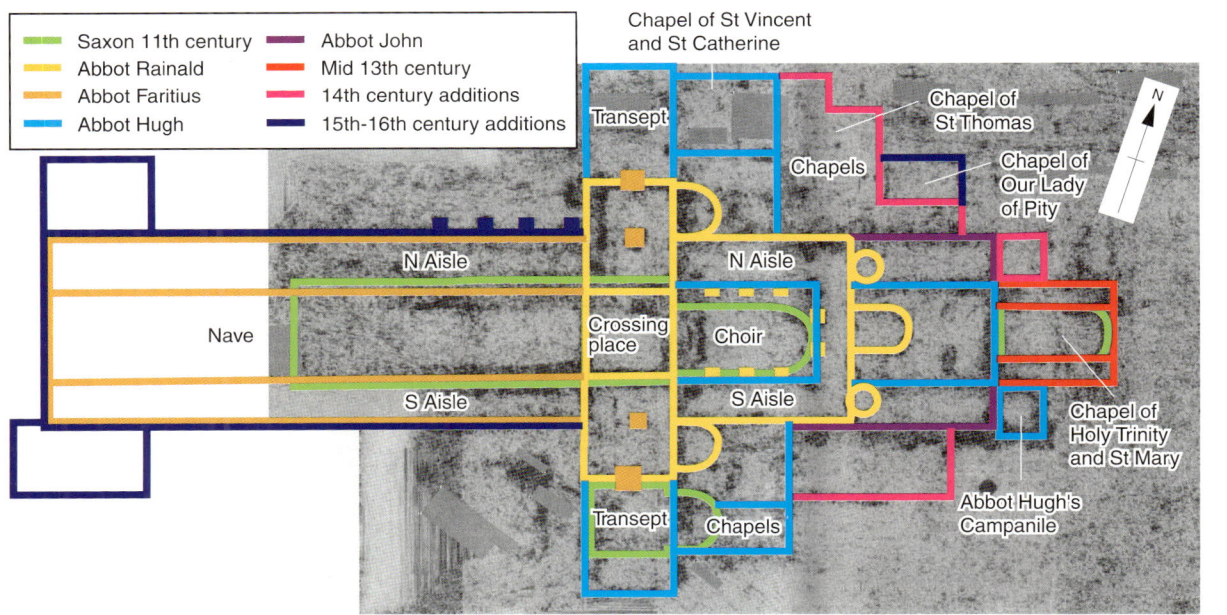

There was less change to the east. A chapel of Our Lady of Pity was built shortly before the Dissolution. Its whereabouts is uncertain, but we have shown it north of the choir.

17

Organisation of the Abbey

The building programme could not have happened without considerable revenues. These came from property granted by the king or other benefactors as acts of piety. In return, the king expected the abbey to supply and finance knights and men-at-arms for his wars, and all benefactors expected the monks to pray to God on their behalf. In the Catholic faith of medieval England, the dead waited in purgatory, paying for their sins, before being admitted to heaven, and masses said by the monks could shorten this.

The head of the abbey was the abbot, for whom a number of estates catered directly. He was a great magnate, often involved in politics, with his own courtyard of buildings west of the cloister including state apartments for visiting royalty and nobles. The daily management of the abbey was left to the Prior, assisted by a sub-prior and a third prior. By the 12th century, the prior had a group of senior monks (called obedientiaries), each responsible for one aspect of the abbey's needs. There were also wardens for the various chapels. The main building programme – the Great Work – was however managed by the Treasurer, responsible directly to the abbot.

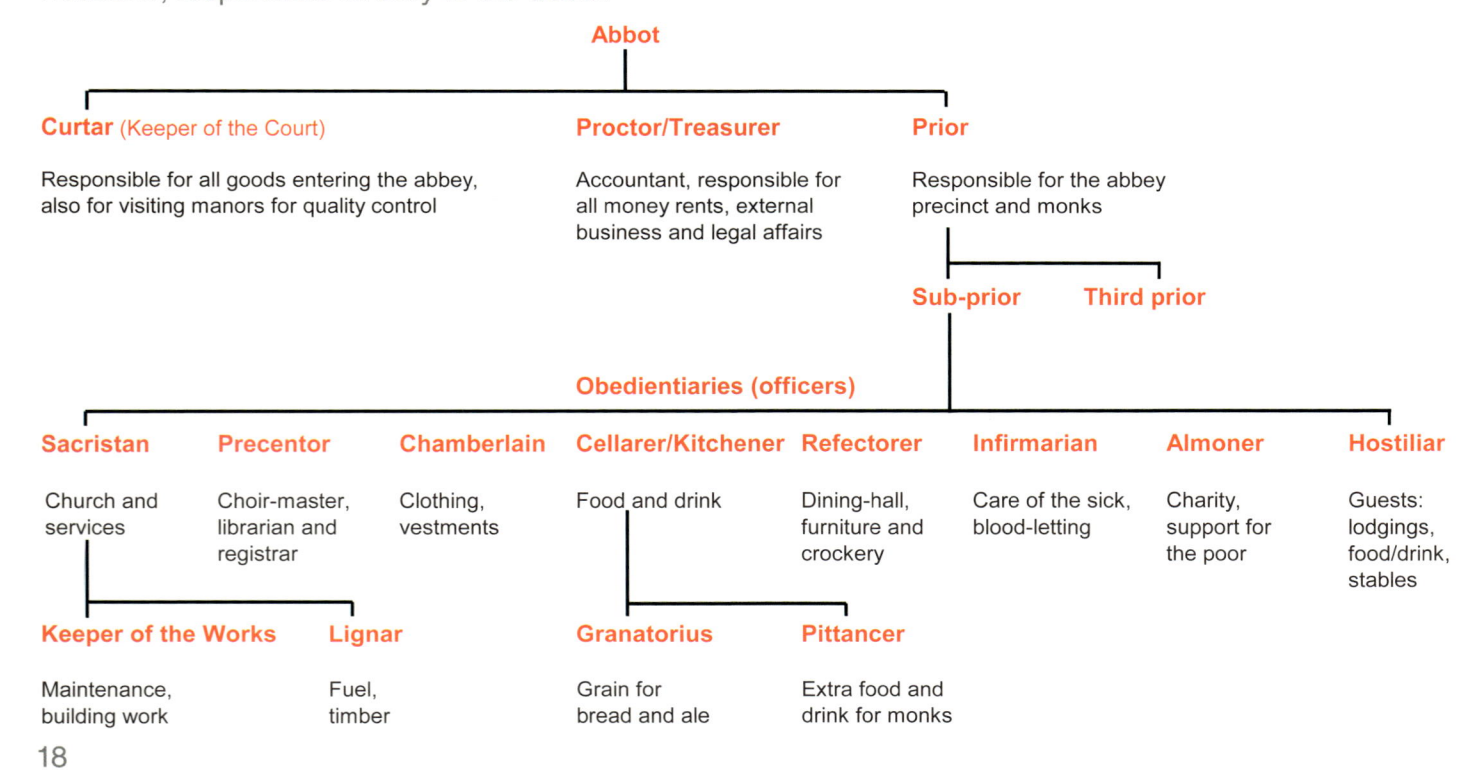

Abbot

Curtar (Keeper of the Court)
Responsible for all goods entering the abbey, also for visiting manors for quality control

Proctor/Treasurer
Accountant, responsible for all money rents, external business and legal affairs

Prior
Responsible for the abbey precinct and monks

Sub-prior **Third prior**

Obedientiaries (officers)

Sacristan	**Precentor**	**Chamberlain**	**Cellarer/Kitchener**	**Refectorer**	**Infirmarian**	**Almoner**	**Hostiliar**
Church and services	Choir-master, librarian and registrar	Clothing, vestments	Food and drink	Dining-hall, furniture and crockery	Care of the sick, blood-letting	Charity, support for the poor	Guests: lodgings, food/drink, stables

Keeper of the Works
Maintenance, building work

Lignar
Fuel, timber

Granatorius
Grain for bread and ale

Pittancer
Extra food and drink for monks

The Abbey as landowner

The abbey estates were concentrated in North Berkshire (now Oxfordshire), with outliers in Windsor Forest, on the Chilterns and in the Cotswolds. Most of these practised mixed farming, but the Vale of White Horse estates provided most of the grain and the dairy farms, those in Windsor Forest timber and pigs, though there were also woodlands on the downs and in the Thames valley. There were river-fisheries along the rivers Thames and Ock. The estates on the Downs, Chilterns and Cotswolds provided sheep, as did estates on the Corallian ridge in the Thames valley. Stone was quarried at Wheatley, Cumnor and Bayworth, and the Cotswolds were also a source of stone.

Seven of the manors —Cumnor, Barton (in Abingdon itself), Marcham, Charney, Uffington, Lockinge and Milton - were devoted solely to the feeding of the monastery. Originally most of the manors were required to send produce to the abbey, but over time this was changed to money payments, the goods themselves being sold in local markets.

Abingdon Abbey estates (after James Bond, published Landscape Archaeology 1979)

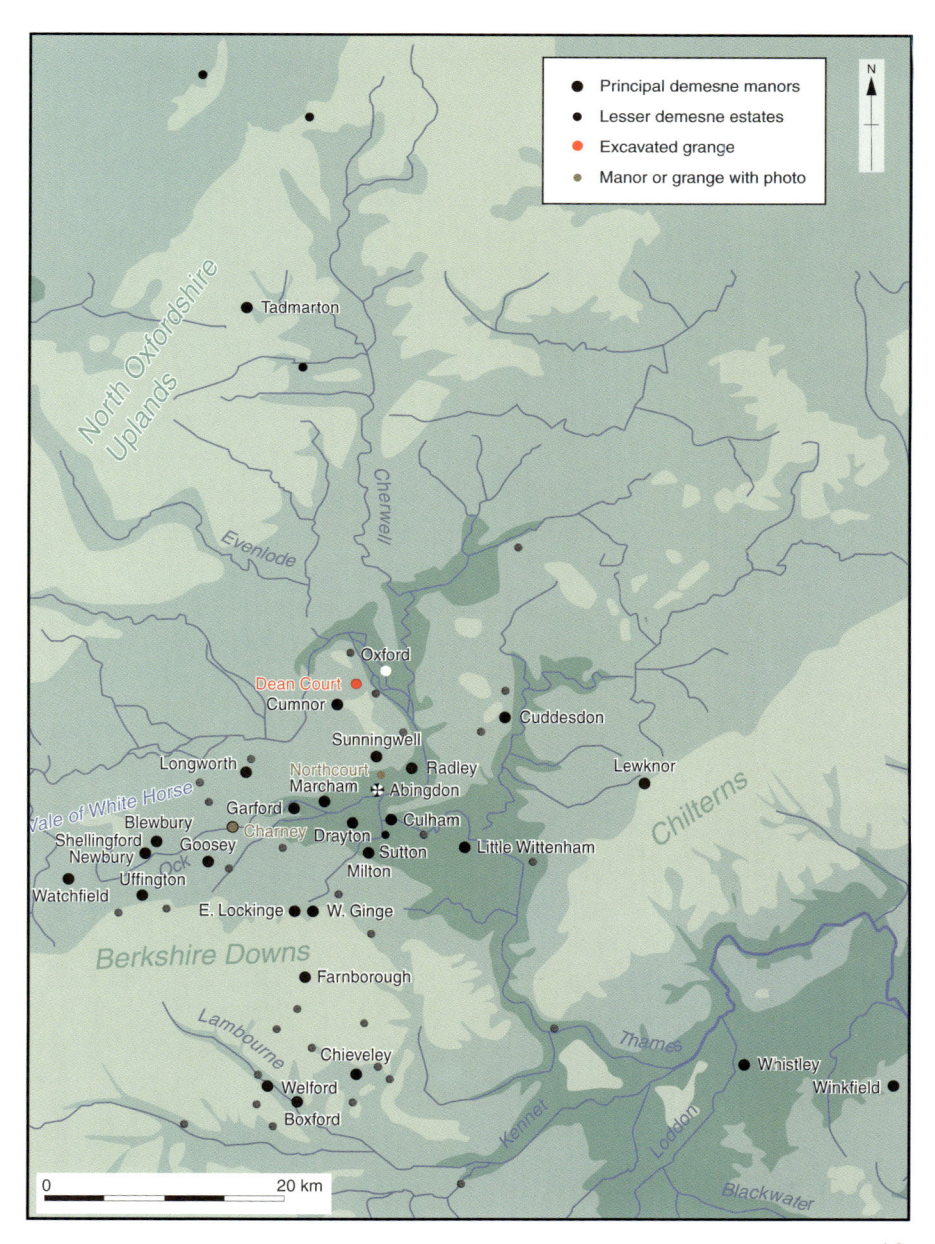

The abbey properties: the Base Court and the Barton

The abbey had a Base Court south of the cloister, to which supplies for immediate consumption were delivered. Those visiting the abbey on business, and their horses, were also housed there. Here there were barns, granaries, and stables, the malt house, brewery and bakehouse, with the corn mills and fulling mills adjacent. The land within the precinct north of the church and lay cemetery contained orchards, walled gardens and vegetable plots. The obedentiars accounts record apples, some for cider, pears, nuts and onions. Beyond these was the Vineyard (south of the road of that name), first mentioned in documents in AD 1185, and still producing wine until the 15th century.

East of the abbey was the Barton or home farm, where a large barn housed the estate's stores, and to which produce from the local fields was taken. The Barton was originally located just north-east of the precinct, south of the Vineyard road and west of Barton Lane. It was burnt in the riots of AD 1327 (see page 29), and later rebuilt east of Barton Lane. The Monks' Map shows several of the buildings, including a circular dovecote (see detail below). Resistivity and magnetometer surveys were carried out by Roger Ainslie around the surviving ruin, showing walls to the south but not very clearly. Barton Court was burnt down again during the English Civil War, but a ruin still remains. Later drawings and pictures show that it was rebuilt further south, straddling the lane.

Detail of Monks' Map (Copyright Abingdon Town Council)

Part of the manor house at Charney Bassett (Copyright Ann Berkeley)

Manors and granges of Abingdon Abbey

The properties belonging to the abbey were administered in several different ways. Some were long-established manors with their own village and fields, such as Fitzharris, or Charney Bassett, with its own fields leased to local noblemen, who paid a proportion of the produce (or a cash alternative) to the abbey every year. At Fitzharris all that is left of the manor is the Norman castle mound or motte by the Stert (see photo on right). At Charney Bassett, however, much of the medieval manor house is still standing.

Others, called granges (literally meaning barns), were run directly by the abbey through an overseer called a reeve. One of these was at Northcourt (less than a mile from the home farm at Barton), where a fine barn still survives (see below) . The foundations of a much larger barn were found recently at Cumnor.

There were twelve such granges in Cumnor parish, an extensive system of directly-managed abbey farms. Some were newly created in the 12th century by `assarting', that is clearing woodland. By the end of the 14th century most of the abbey's farms were let to tenants for cash rents, though Cumnor itself remained a retreat for the monks until the Dissolution, when the abbot retired there.

The grange at Dean Court Farm

The more distant granges also had domestic buildings. One of these, at Dean Court in Cumnor parish, has been excavated. The plan shows the first, 13th century, grange, which was found when the Cumnor bypass was constructed. It consisted of an L-shaped house of two storeys with a byre or cattle shed at one end (the upper floor ran over the passage and byre), and two barns surrounded by ditches. The barns, similar in size to that at Northcourt, were better built than the house, showing the priorities of the abbey that ran the grange.

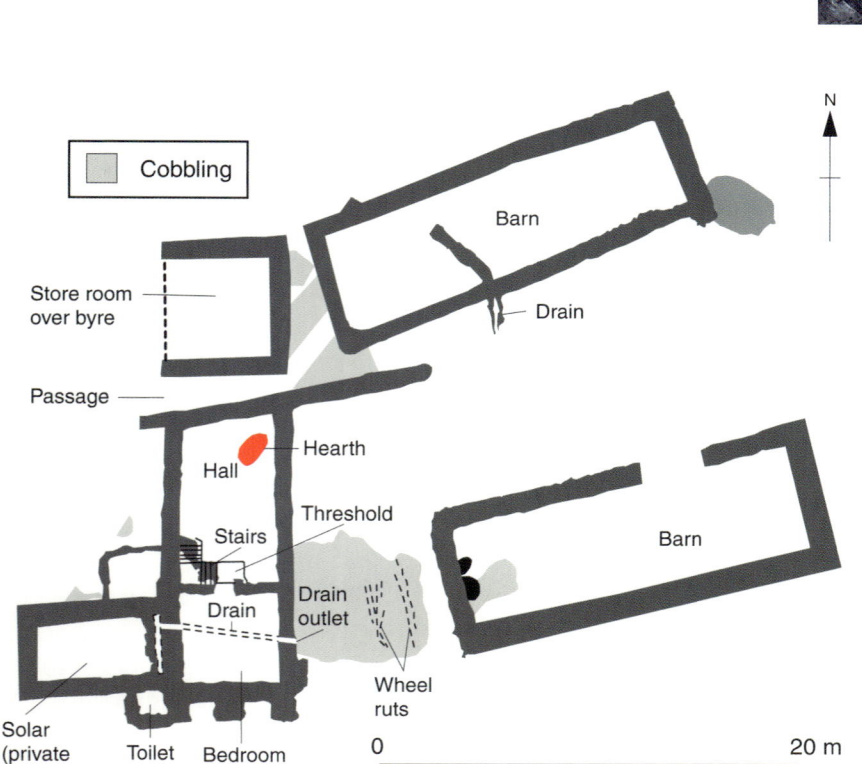

14th century kitchen showing ovens (top) and stone channel and fish tanks

The grange moved to the valley bottom in the early 14th century, presumably to aid the construction of a moat for protection. At this time famine and a weak king led to lawlessness (see page 29), so moats were common, but fish were also farmed here, as an elaborate system of tanks in the kitchen shows. A later survey of the manor of Wookey in Somerset describes a similar arrangement: `oon close yarde wythe water ronnynge throughte and walled about wythe 2 stone trowes for to kepe and water fyshe in yt..' *(Devon R.O. [Exeter], Rolle papers 96M/Box 4/5, Survey 1557-8. Transcript by Joan Hasler).*

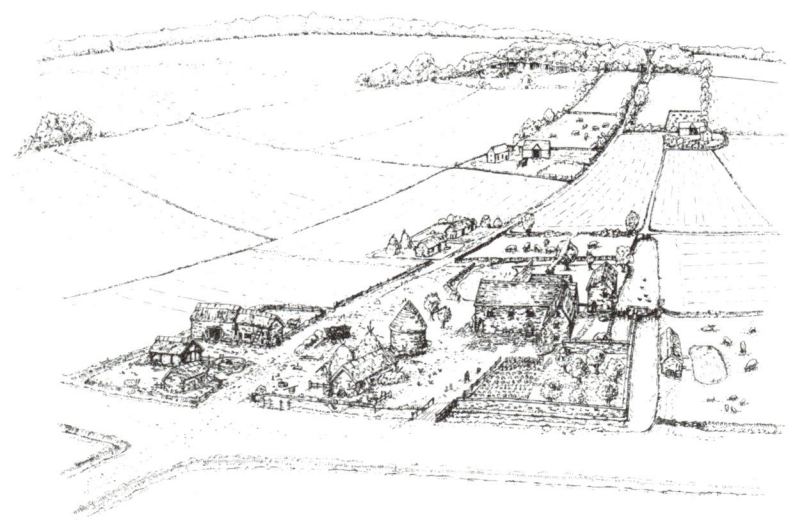

Reconstruction by Harry Lange and Danyon Rey of OA

Surviving solar with blocked medieval windows

The reconstruction shows the probable layout in the 14th century. The domestic buildings (of which one wing survives – see photo) were arranged like those of other manors, not set out around a cloister. Documents also mention a separate grange church (*ecclesia*), but this has not been found.

Foundations of the circular dovecote under excavation

The foundations of a dovecote were excavated at Dean Court. Annual grange accounts record the vast numbers of eggs and birds supplied to the abbey. Dovecotes were the privilege of the wealthy, and limited to manor-owners or monasteries.

Farm labourers lived in cottages in adjacent plots (tofts) alongside the lane. One of the cottagers had a kiln in the backyard, and many jugs were discarded into the ditches around it, suggesting that the owner had brewed ale as a sideline.

Fish

Monks' Map (Copyright Abingdon Town Council)

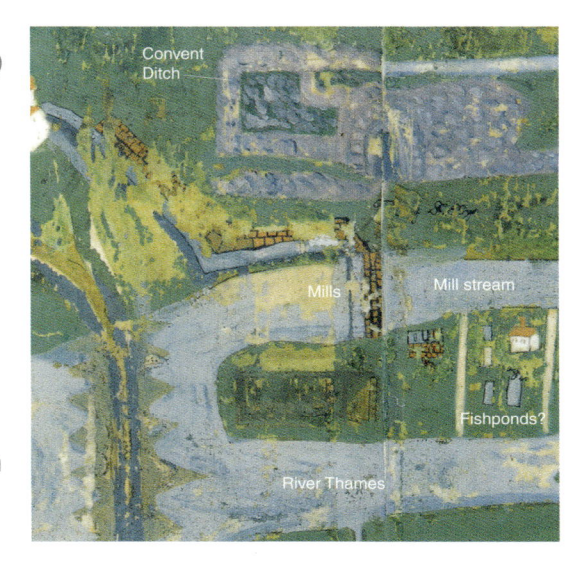

Fish was very important in the monastic diet, and both salt and freshwater fish were eaten. Abingdon Abbey farmed fish within the precinct; the Pittancer's Account of AD 1322 records the stocking of a new fishpond. Names on the 16th century Monks' Map include Fish House Close, Great Pond Close and Brewern Hays Close in what is now Abbey Meadows. This low-lying area was probably where abbey fishponds used to be.

Sales of fish from the Convent Ditch in the town market are recorded in the 15th century accounts. The Convent Ditch, which appears on the Monks' Map, surrounded the north and west sides of the church, and was partly excavated west of Abbey House (see page 14). It was 12 m wide and 2 m deep, and was fed by the river Stert to the north. A wooden bridge was later built across it for access to an orchard behind Stert Street. Matching the tree-ring patterns of the oak bridge timbers (dendrochronology) has shown that it was built in AD 1507.

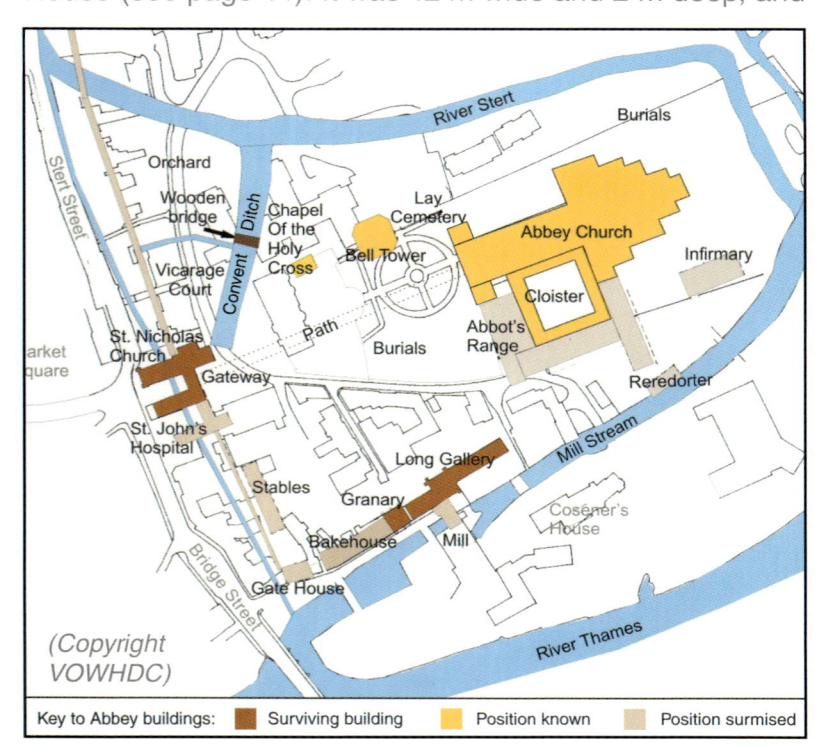

Waterlogged timbers from two wooden trestles that supported a bridge across the moat or Convent Ditch. The upper parts were above the level of the water table and so have not survived.

Daisy Banks: Abbey Causeway or Fishpond?

The Nature Reserve contains earthworks thought to have been Abbey fishponds, though ownership by the Abbey is not proven. The valley is fed by two streams, and is crossed by a high earth bank, which carried the road to Radley until the early 20th century. There are smaller banks along the valley sides (see sketch plan), and a net-sinker has been found here. Together these all indicate a fishpond.

The AAAHS dug a trench to investigate its construction, (see section below). First the topsoil was removed, and then gravel dug from either side to start the mound. A vertical division between the layers along the edge and in the middle probably marks wooden shuttering (now decayed), supported by gravel thrown up on the outer side. Wooden uprights were also driven in along the edge of the bank to stop it slipping; one was preserved below the water table. The middle was filled with layers of compacted soil, gravel and clay a metre deep. The bank was capped with rammed gravel to form a roadway, and a stone sluice was built where the stream crosses the bank. Unfortunately there were no finds, so its date is still uncertain. Sometime between the 14th and 18th centuries the bank was heightened again. Snails identified in the silt upstream of the bank were all terrestrial, suggesting that it was not permanently wet, but the silt was not dated.

The excavations have shown that the bank was used as a causeway to cross the boggy valley from the start. As this linked Abingdon Abbey to its manor at Radley, the abbey was probably responsible for building the bank.

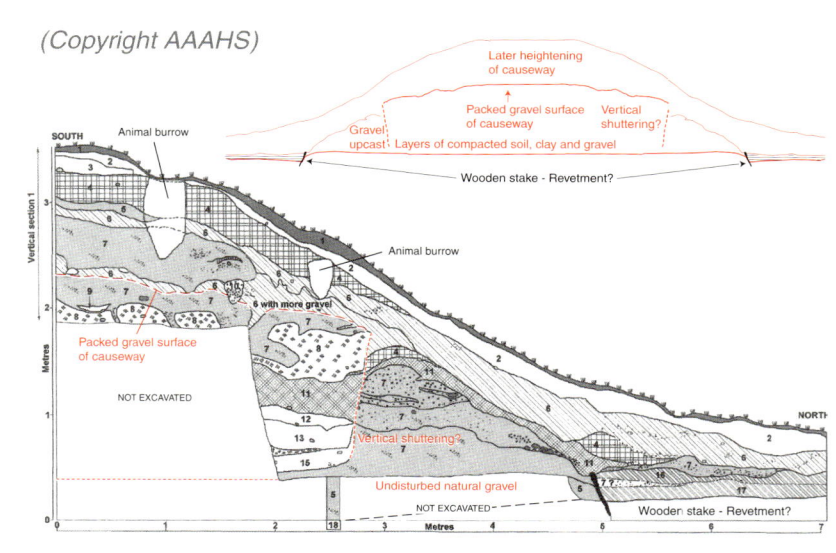

(Copyright James Bond)

(Copyright AAAHS)

The Abbey and the town

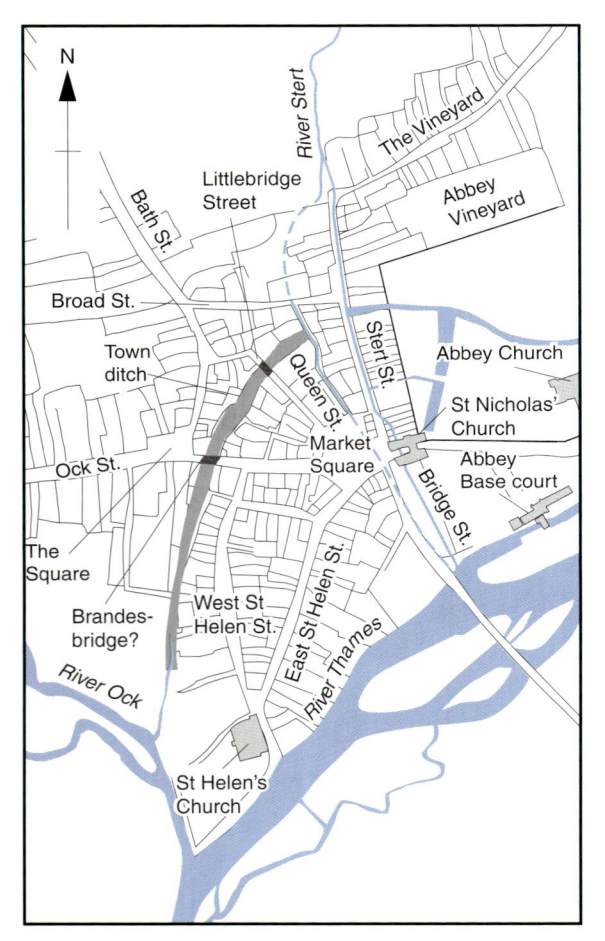

The Domesday Book (AD 1086) tells us of "ten merchants dwelling in front of the church gate". The right to hold a weekly market was granted by Edward the Confessor and confirmed by Henry I (AD 1107-1128). However, the reign of Henry II saw a long-running legal dispute between the Abbey and Wallingford over its rights to hold a market. On one occasion the men of Wallingford tried to break up the market, but were routed by the Abbey's retainers. Eventually the King confirmed the abbey's right to hold a full weekly market.

Abingdon Abbey controlled markets and fairs in the town, charging stallholders and policing them (see also pages 27-8). Taxes and dues were collected in the guildhall in the Market Square. We now know that there were probably three entrances through the defences, with open areas for livestock markets just outside each one. Brandesbridge is recorded just east of St Edmund's chapel, so may have crossed the ditch just east of the Square. In medieval times Bury Street was known as Little Bridge Street, ie leading to a bridge over the town ditch. There is a square just outside, formerly the site of a horsefair. Stert Street too widens just north of the line of the ditch, and this is a common sign of a former market area. Markets continued to be held in all three areas in post-medieval times.

18th century engraving of St Nicholas church from the north, showing the open Stert Stream alongside Stert Street (courtesy Friends of Abingdon)

The Abbey's new development in the town

Other abbeys promoted the development of the towns around them, both to increase revenues and to improve the lives of their dependents. We now think that Abingdon Abbey did the same in the late 12th century AD. The `old' river Stert had previously run down Queen Street, but a new straight channel (still existing but now covered over) was now dug down Stert Street, passing under a new church, St Nicholas, and a new almshouse for the poor, St John's Hospital, either side of the abbey gateway.

The new channel (see engraving page 26) was probably to provide water for new properties between it and the abbey precinct all along the east side of Stert Street. Throughout the medieval period these properties were owned by the Abbey, and were almost all rented by abbey servants (employees). St Nicholas was their parish church.

The new development may have included the properties on the south side of the Vineyard. The abbey vineyard is first mentioned in AD 1185, and was probably laid out, together with the tenements between it and the road, around this time. There have been excavations all along the Vineyard recently in advance of redevelopment, and these suggest a similar late 12th century start date. The Vineyard is very wide here, and the abbey may have planned a local marketplace here to support its new suburb.

Photograph of the Abbey gateway with St Nicholas church on the left and St John's Hospital on the right

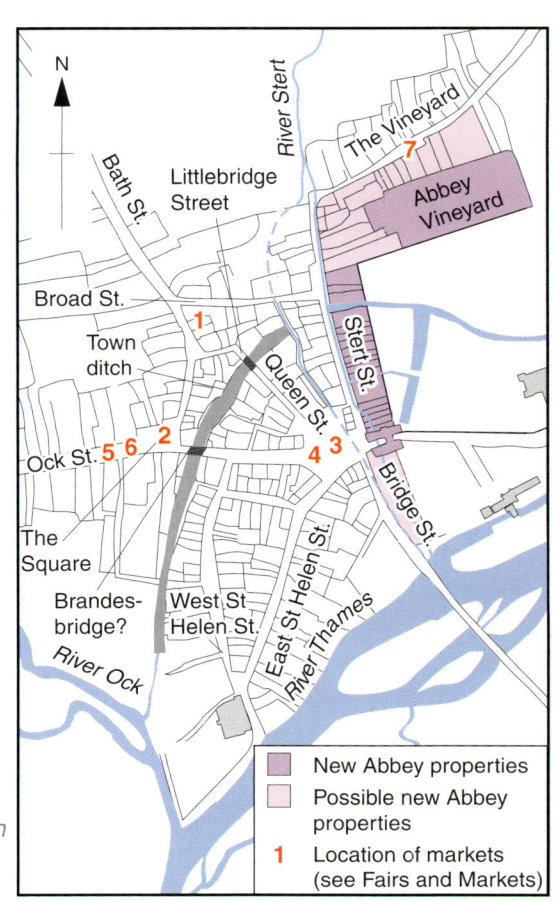

27

Abingdon fairs and markets

As well as a regular market, there were also fairs. Abingdon's earliest fairs were all associated with religious festivals. The greatest was that of St. Mary, to whom the abbey was dedicated. Centred on her feast day on 8th September, it was ranked among the five greatest fairs in the country. Merchants from all over Europe came for the Abbey's fine wool, and a livestock market was also included. St Margaret's and Lent fairs were smaller.

In AD 1290 King Edward I granted a charter for St. Edmund's fair, held around his feast day, to raise money for the upkeep of St. Edmund's Chapel. Unusually it lasted for seven days. St. Andrew's fair was granted in AD 1520 to the Fraternity of the Holy Cross by King Henry VIII. Both were pleasure fairs with a livestock market.

Fair	Origin	Duration	Purpose	Location
Lent	12/13th century	Monday (early March)		1
St Edmunds	AD 1290	6th-12th June	Pleasure/livestock	2
St Margarets	12/13th century	12nd-14th July	Livestock	3
St Mary's	12th century	7th-9th September	Wool/livestock	4
Michaelmas	AD 1349	Monday end September	Hiring/pleasure	5
Runaway	AD 1350	1st Monday October	Hiring/pleasure	6
St Andrews	AD 1520	29Nov-1st Dec	Pleasure/livestock	7

Following the Black Death there was an acute shortage of agricultural labour, resulting in ever-higher wages. To regulate this, Parliament passed a statute in AD 1349 requiring the Justices of the Peace to decide on a fixed wage for their county. The new wage rates were announced on a Statute or Sessions day in the largest market towns, to which farm workers flocked. In Abingdon this was the Monday before Michaelmas, and this became a hiring fair. If the labourer was not happy with his new employment there was another hiring fair (the Runaway fair) a week later.

When the English calendar was revised in AD 1752 to bring it into line with most European countries, eleven days were lost, and with them the links between the fairs and the religious festivals.

The riots of AD 1327

In AD 1327 King Edward II was deposed, leaving the country in turmoil. There were riots against the great Benedictine abbeys by discontented townspeople, including at Abingdon, due to longstanding grievances held by merchants and tradesmen about market and fair tolls. The townspeople gathered in St Helen's church, destroyed the guildhall and attacked the abbey gateway, but were repelled, 2 people being killed.

A few days later an Oxford mob, including the mayor and corporation and students, burnt the abbey's granges at Barton and Northcourt, and, joining the townspeople of Abingdon, attacked the abbey. From the Barton one group entered by a small gate into the Pittancery, then into the lay cemetery, and let in those attacking the main gate. Many monks, including the abbot, fled across the river by boat, and some drowned. The rioters killed one monk at the high altar, and `burned what buildings they could'. They looted anything of portable value, and destroyed many abbey documents and others deposited by local landowners for safekeeping.

The prior (the abbot's deputy) was made to sign a document absolving the rioters and a charter granting them the right to govern the town. When the abbot returned with an armed escort, however, many of them were arrested, and 12 were hanged at Wallingford castle.

(Copyright Barry Samuels, http://www.beenthere-donethat.org.uk)

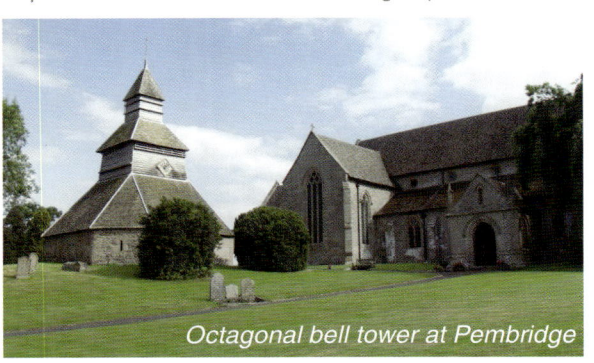

Octagonal bell tower at Pembridge

Physical evidence of the riots was found in the excavations under Abbey House. The stone and mortar foundations of the belltower in the lay cemetery were burnt pink (see photo above), and a worn coin of around AD 1300 was found in the backfill of the robbing of the surrounding octagonal wall (see surviving example on left). This wooden building is likely to have been one of those burnt in 1327.

It was probably because of the riots that the western arm of the Convent Ditch moat was dug from the Stert down to the abbey gateway east of St Nicolas' church (see page 16).

29

Town Enterprise, Charity and Relief of the Poor

Painting of the Market Cross in the Long Alley almshouses AD 1607

St John's Hospital, built in the 12th century, stood immediately outside the Abbey Gateway. It cared for the sick, poor, and travellers. In later medieval times religious organisations in the town shared or took over services provided by the abbey, and by the 16th century St John's Hospital was being used as an almshouse for six aged monastic employees.

(Copyright Christ's Hospital)

(Photos copyright Ann Berkeley)

The Fraternity of the Holy Cross was a religious guild comprised largely of rich merchants associated with St Helen's Church, where it supported two chaplains. In AD 1416 two of its members (see above) obtained a licence to build the bridges at Abingdon and Culham with a connecting causeway across the flood meadows of the Thames. This ensured Abingdon's place on the lucrative wool trade route from London to the West Country. Soon after obtaining a Royal Charter in AD 1441 the Fraternity erected a great stone cross in the Market Place. Described by John Leland as "a right goodly crosse of stone", it was destroyed in AD 1644 by Waller's Parliamentarian troops during the Civil War.

In AD 1446 the Fraternity of the Holy Cross built the Long Alley Almshouse next to St Helen's church, and members commonly left properties in their will to provide rents for its upkeep. The hospital provided relief for thirteen poor people, seven men and six women, who initially received 1d per week. St Helen's supported the residents of the "old Almshouse" (later the Brick Alley almshouses), and there would have been parish doles and collections for the poor.

After the Abbey

At the dissolution the abbot was granted Cumnor Place for life, and the prior and the 24 monks all received generous pensions. The king considered using the abbot's lodgings himself (and saving part of the church as his chapel), but the monks had sold or taken everything but the bare buildings, and refurbishment was judged too expensive. The lay cemetery was closed.

(Photo copyright Ann Berkeley)

The church was gradually demolished, much stone being shipped downriver to build palaces at Westminster and Oatlands, Surrey. In AD 1553 the stone of the central tower was sold to build a new mansion at Barton, shown on the Monks' Map. The surviving ruin belongs to this. The abbot's lodging and the infirmary were the last to go, in around AD 1579. Ironically, the medieval ruin erected by Trendell in the Abbey Gardens in Victorian times probably comes not from the long-demolished abbey, but from St Helen's Church, which was altered while his Abbey Gardens were being constructed.

The manors that had supported the abbey were given away by the king. The abbey site itself was looked after by a `keeper' until AD 1553, when it was sold to William Blacknall, a miller. The tomb of his son John and wife Mary is in St Nicholas' church. Their daughter Mary married Sir Ralph Verney, and the `Verney papers' are the main records about the site until the end of the English Civil War. They include a second 16th century map of Abingdon (see next page).

The Monks' Map shows demolition in progress, with only the west end of the church visible, and much of the Convent Ditch filled in. Blacknall fell out with the vicar of St Nicholas, and filled in the boundary ditch between them; the infill was found during the 1989 excavations.

The Verney 16th century map has no trace of the church, but shows two substantial (but stylised) houses within the former precinct. One was possibly the abbot's lodging, the other probably `Master Stone's Lodging' (brother-in-law of the last abbot) just inside the Abbey Gateway. The Blacknalls made this their home, and later rebuilt it in stone. It is now Old Abbey House.

One of the houses may alternatively be the Cosener's (the medieval kitchener's) Inn, a large riverside house at the bottom of Abbey Close. William Blacknall purchased it as part of the abbey site, but did not live there, although he kept a dovecote and a small orchard. As this and later maps show, most of the abbey site remained as gardens, orchards, pasture and meadows.

(Copyright Verney Papers Maps 12/1/127)

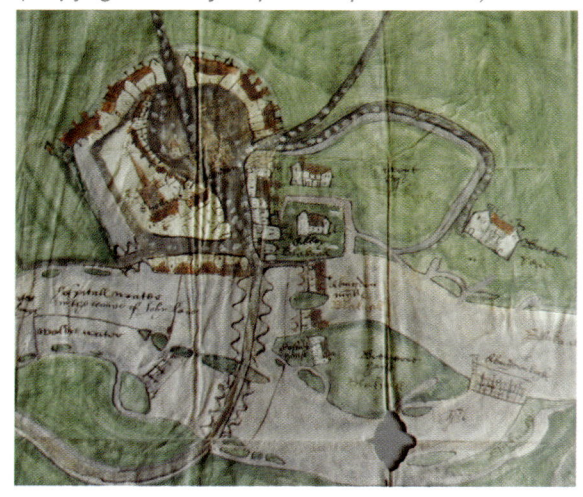

During the English Civil War the abbey gateway was used as a military prison, and after execution prisoners and others were buried in the orchard north of the vicarage. All of the graves were north-south (see excavation photo). There was room for east-west burials, and there was no bishop's licence for this cemetery, perhaps indicating a low-church Parliamentarian origin. More than half of the 400 graves found in the excavations contained men of military age. Some were probably from the Parliamentarian army, others Royalists, like the 9 men from the prison buried in one grave (photo on right). Others were women and children, probably victims of typhus and other diseases spread by the armies. The cemetery went out of use after the Restoration of Charles 2nd, and was rapidly forgotten.

Despite the wholesale demolition of the abbey, buildings were still commonly described as "in the Abbey" until the 20th century.